W9-CLA-389

HURRICANES

Earth's Power

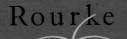

David and Patricia Armentrout

Rourke
Publishing LLC
Vero Beach, Florida 32964

www.rourkepublishing.com

PHOTO CREDITS: Cover, pg 7 ©Photodisc, Inc.; Title pg, pgs 12, 23 courtesy of the USCG; Pg 5 ©Megan Williamson; Pg 9 ©Fred Green; Pg 10 inset courtesy of NASA; Pgs 7 inset, 10, 14, 14 inset, 26 courtesy of NOAA/Department of Commerce; Pgs 13, 18 inset courtesy of the Department of Defense; Pg 17 inset courtesy of the Library of Congress; Pgs 17, 18, 21, 21 inset, 22, 24, 25, 28, 29 courtesy of FEMA

Title page: Hurricanes have strong winds that cause high and dangerous seas.

Editor: Robert Stengard-Olliges

Cover and page design by Nicola Stratford

Library of Congress Cataloging-in-Publication Data

Armentrout, David, 1962-
  Hurricanes / David and Patricia Armentrout.
     p. cm. -- (Earth's power)
  Includes index.
  ISBN 1-60044-232-3
  1. Hurricanes--Juvenile literature. I. Armentrout, Patricia, 1960- II.
Title. III. Series: Armentrout, David, 1962- Earth's power.

  QC944.2.A76 2007
  551.55'2--dc22

2006011094

Printed in the USA

Rourke Publishing
1-800-394-7055
www.rourkepublishing.com
sales@rourkepublishing.com
Post Office Box 3328, Vero Beach, FL 32964

TABLE OF CONTENTS

HURRICANE SEASON

For many people, the summer season is a time to celebrate. The air is warm, the days are long, and it is the perfect time to play in the ocean waves. But summer can cause some people to become uneasy, especially those living along the coast. Why? Summer is hurricane season.

A hurricane is a huge, **tropical** cyclone. Cyclone is a term **meteorologists** use to describe a rotating windstorm.

The term *hurricane* is specific to storms that form in the North Atlantic Ocean, the Northeast Pacific Ocean and the Southeast Pacific Ocean. *Tropical cyclone* is the term used for storms in the Indian Ocean, while *typhoon* describes storms in the Northwest Pacific Ocean.

4

Warm ocean waters attract tourists, but they can also fuel hurricanes.

Thunderstorms often form from

tall dense cloud clusters.

Hurricanes grow from strong tropical thunderstorms.

BORN IN THE TROPICS

A hurricane does not start out as a monster storm; it forms from a tropical disturbance—a large area of organized thunderstorms. A tropical disturbance can grow into a tropical **depression**, or area of low pressure, with circulating winds up to 38 miles (61 km) an hour.

A tropical depression forms when warm ocean water heats moist air above it and causes the air to rise. Cool, dense air moves in and replaces the warm air.

TROPICAL STORMS

A tropical depression becomes a tropical storm when winds reach 39 miles (62 km) an hour. This is when a storm is named. Naming storms makes it easier to communicate information between hurricane forecasters and the public, especially if more than one storm threatens an area at the same time.

A palm tree bends against strong tropical winds.

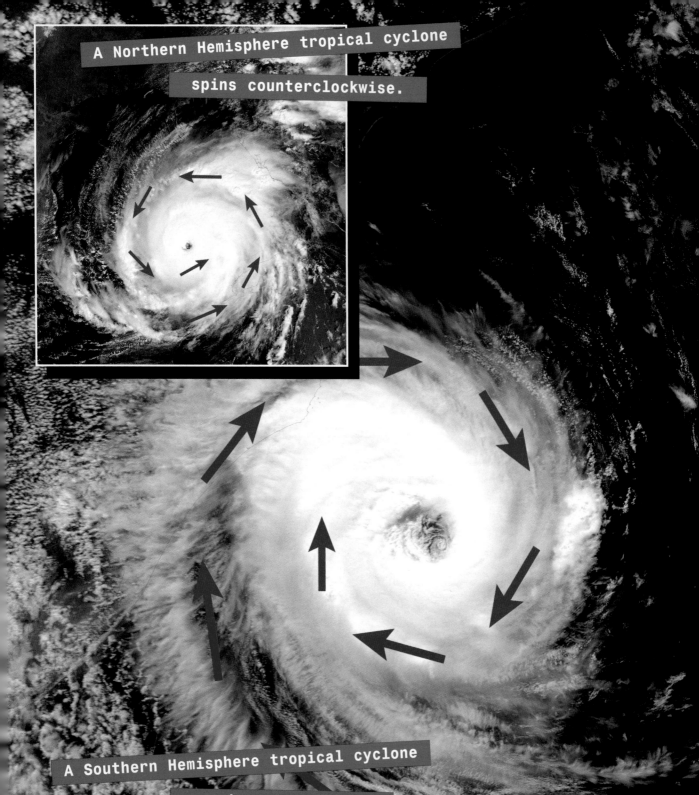

A Northern Hemisphere tropical cyclone spins counterclockwise.

A Southern Hemisphere tropical cyclone spins clockwise.

CORIOLIS EFFECT

Did you know tropical cyclones in the Northern Hemisphere spin counter-clockwise, or to the left, but spin in the opposite direction in the Southern Hemisphere? This is because the earth's rotation has an effect on wind and air pressure. The effect is called the **Coriolis effect**.

The Coriolis effect is greatest at the poles and zero at the equator. Without the Coriolis effect, cyclones cannot form.

1780-The Great Hurricane:

"The Great Hurricane" swept through the Lesser Antilles in the Caribbean Sea. The powerful storm took an estimated 22,000 lives, more than in any other Atlantic hurricane.

HURRICANE STRENGTH

When a tropical storm reaches 74 miles (119 km) an hour it becomes a hurricane. If a hurricane travels away from warm waters, or over land, it loses energy and eventually weakens and dies.

An oil platform tilts to one side after Hurricane Dennis moved through the Gulf of Mexico.

HURRICANES NEED SPECIFIC CONDITIONS IN ORDER TO FORM

- A tropical disturbance
- Distance of at least 300 miles (483 km) from the equator
- Ocean water at least 80°F (26.7° C)
- Moist air
- Little change in wind direction at all levels of the atmosphere

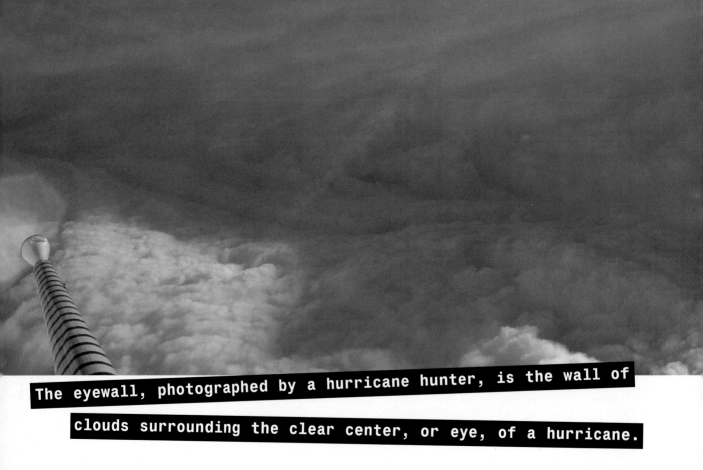

Hurricane winds blow debris through the air with incredible force.

The eyewall, photographed by a hurricane hunter, is the wall of clouds surrounding the clear center, or eye, of a hurricane.

HURRICANE PARTS

A hurricane is made up of three main parts, the eye, the eyewall, and the rainbands. The eye is the somewhat calm, clear center. The eyewall is a column of clouds surrounding the eye. It has the highest **sustained** wind speeds.

Sometimes the eyewall will become very small, allowing outer rainbands to form a second eyewall. This is known as a **concentric eyewall** cycle. This typically happens as a storm weakens. However, a second eyewall can steal the energy of the first and eventually replace it, allowing the hurricane to regain strength.

Hurricane rainbands consist of spiraling thunderstorms. They produce heavy rains and strong winds that often spawn tornadoes. Rainbands can extend 300 miles (483 km) from the eye.

Meteorologists use a hurricane rating system called the Saffir-Simpson Scale. The scale uses wind speed to describe the intensity of a storm and to help estimate potential damage.

SAFFIR-SIMPSON SCALE

- Category One Hurricane:Winds 74-95 mph (119-153km/hr)
- Category Two Hurricane:Winds 96-110 mph (154-177 km/hr)
- Category Three Hurricane:Winds 111-130 mph (178-209 km/hr)
- Category Four Hurricane:Winds 131-155 mph (210-249 km/hr)
- Category Five Hurricane:Winds greater than 155 mph (249 km/hr)

A house sits atop debris deposited by the 1900 Galveston hurricane.

A Category Four hurricane leaves a path of destruction as far as the eye can see.

Hurricanes often flood areas leaving survivors trapped and in need of rescue.

Hurricane Ivan's storm surge left huge amounts of sand and debris in this Florida home.

LIVING IN DANGER ZONES

Each year more and more people move closer to the coast. They are drawn by warm temperatures, beautiful beaches, and of course, the ocean. Unfortunately, this means many people are now living in hurricane danger zones.

Hurricanes bring heavy rains that flood low-lying areas. They have fierce winds that uproot trees and damage buildings. They also produce a **storm surge**—a huge wall of ocean water caused by wind. As a hurricane makes **landfall**, the storm surge moves inland, carrying massive amounts of sand and debris. Strong hurricanes can redefine coastlines and leave total destruction in their wake.

Storm prediction centers exist to issue hurricane watches and warnings, and provide information on hurricane preparedness. People living in danger zones can learn how to secure their home, put together a disaster supply kit, and learn how and where to **evacuate** if necessary.

Evacuation shelters are located away from the coast. They can be in churches, schools, or large auditoriums. During Hurricane Katrina in 2005, the Louisiana Superdome and the New Orleans convention center became emergency evacuation shelters for thousands of people displaced by the storm.

ERNEST N. MORIAL
CONVENTION CENTER NEW ORLEANS

HURRICANE EVACUATION ROUTE

Road signs clearly mark hurricane evacuation routes in coastal areas.

New Orleans residents seek emergency shelter

prior to the landfall of hurricane Katrina.

Neighborhoods in Biloxi, Mississippi suffered extensive damage from hurricane Katrina.

HURRICANE KATRINA 2005

Katrina formed near the Bahamas, and within two days gained hurricane strength and made landfall in southern Florida. Katrina moved into the Gulf of Mexico where it intensified to a Category Five hurricane. Katrina made a second landfall in Louisiana as a Category Three and then crossed Breton Sound making its final landfall in Mississippi.

Two ships are left stranded after Katrina ripped through Louisiana.

A tremendous amount of damage was done to the city of New Orleans. Katrina's fierce winds and storm surge caused the **levees** separating the city from Lake Pontchartrain to **breach**. After the storm passed, 80 percent of New Orleans was under water. Katrina caused catastrophic damage to Louisiana, Mississippi, and Alabama and killed more than 1,300 people. It was the costliest natural disaster to strike the United States, resulting in more than 100 billion dollars in estimated damages.

A hurricane survivor is pulled from floodwater.

New Orleans remained under water for weeks after hurricane Katrina.

Two NOAA aircraft collect weather data using onboard radar and sensors.

HURRICANE

HUNTERS

Can you imagine flying an airplane into some of the worst storms Mother Nature creates? That's what hurricane hunters do. The U. S. Air Force and the National Oceanic and Atmospheric Administration (NOAA) operate teams of hurricane hunters. Their jobs are to fly into tropical storms. Instruments on board special aircraft take measurements and record wind speed and air pressure. Meteorologists use the data to create more accurate forecast models.

Even with detailed information collected by hurricane hunters, forecasters cannot pinpoint where a hurricane will strike. Hurricanes are unpredictable and unstoppable forces of nature. But with advanced computer systems, satellites, and radar, forecasters can better predict a hurricane's path. Improved forecasting gives people more time to get out of harms way.

The path of hurricane Ivan is closely tracked at the National Hurricane Center in Miami.

28

Hurricane Andrew was one of the most destructive hurricanes to hit the U.S.

GLOSSARY

breach (BREECH) — to break through leaving an opening

concentric eyewall (kuhn SEN trik EYE WAWL) — two hurricane eyewalls at the same time

Coriolis effect (KOR ee o less uh FEKT) — the effect of the earth's rotation on wind causing it to follow a curved path

evacuate (ih VAK yoo ate) — to move out of an unsafe location

depression (di PRESH uhn) — in weather, an area of low pressure made up of warm moist air

landfall (LAND FAWL) — the point at which the eye of a hurricane first crosses land

levees (LEV eez) — embankments built to prevent flooding

meteorologists (MEE tee ur OL oh jists) — people who study the atmosphere which causes weather conditions

tropical (TROP uh kuhl) — relating to the tropics which is the area between the Tropic of Cancer (23½ degrees north of the equator) and the Tropic of Capricorn (23½ degrees south of the equator)

storm surge (STORM SERJ) — the rise in sea level that a hurricane or other storm brings, its number is estimated by subtracting the normal high tide level from the storm tide level

sustained (suh STAYND) — maintaining for a period of time without interruption or weakening

FURTHER READING

Chambers, Catherine. *Hurricanes.* Heinemann Library, 2001.

Rotter, Charles. *Hurricanes.* Creative Education, 2003.

Demarest, Chris. *Hurricane Hunters! Riders on the Storm.*
   Margaret K. McElderry, 2006.

WEBSITES TO VISIT

National Hurricane Center
www.nhc.noaa.gov/

National Weather Service
www.nws.noaa.gov

FEMA For Kids
www.fwma.gov/kids/hurr.htm

Hurricane Hunters
www.hurricanehunters.com

INDEX

ABOUT THE AUTHORS

David and Patricia Armentrout have written many nonfiction books for young readers. They have had several books published for primary school reading. The Armentrouts live in Cincinnati, Ohio, with their two children.